P9-CMM-906

AMERICA'S VERY OWN MONSTERS

AMERICA'S VERY OWN MONSTERS

by Daniel Cohen

Illustrated by Tom Huffman

G. P. Putnam's Sons
New York

Library of Congress Cataloging-in-Publication Data
Cohen, Daniel.   America's very own monsters /
by Daniel Cohen : illustrated by Tom Huffman.
p. cm.   Reprint.   Originally published: New York:
Dodd, Mead, © 1982.   Summary: Discusses such creatures
as Bigfoot, the Demon Cat, and Mothman which, though
never proven, are said to exist in the United States.
1. Monsters—United States—Juvenile literature.
[1. Monsters.]   I. Huffman, Tom, ill.   II. Title.
QL89.C6   1989   001.9′44′097—dc19   89-3674   CIP   AC
ISBN 0-399-61249-1
3   5   7   9   10   8   6   4   2

J 133.1
c OH

Contents

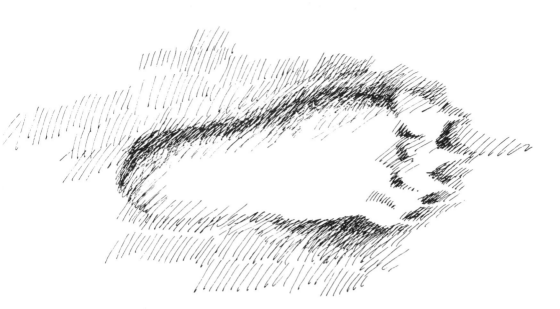

Bigfoot

Jerry Crew runs a bulldozer. He was working in the mountains of Northern California. All the workmen had to camp out. The men heard strange noises at night. Something very large was moving through the trees. It was very near the camp. But no one saw anything.

One night it rained hard. When Jerry Crew woke up he found huge footprints. They were in the mud around the camp. The footprints looked like ones made by a man. But they were nearly twice as big.

Jerry Crew thought that America's best-known monster was at the camp. America's best-known monster is Bigfoot.

Bigfoot is a huge hairy creature. It is anywhere from seven to nine feet tall. It weighs 300 to 400 pounds. Some people say that Bigfoot looks like a giant ape. Others think it looks more like a man.

Most Bigfoot stories come from the states of Washington, Oregon, and Northern California. Some people say that Bigfoot is like the Abominable Snowman. That is a big hairy creature in the mountains of Asia.

Is there really a monster like Bigfoot? The answer depends on whom you talk to. If you asked Jerry Crew, he would say yes. You could ask hundreds of others who say they have seen Bigfoot or its footprints. They will say yes, too.

Most scientists would say there is no such crea-

ture. They would say that Bigfoot stories are just made up. And that the footprints are fakes. Scientists don't see how such a large animal could hide so well. No one has ever been able to catch one. No Bigfoot bones or skin have ever been found.

There is not even a good Bigfoot photograph.

Some monster hunters took what they said was a movie of Bigfoot. That was in 1972. The pictures show a large hairy thing walking through the woods. It could be Bigfoot. But it could also be a man in a monkey suit. There is no way to prove the film is real or fake.

If you want to believe in Bigfoot, that's just fine. If you don't want to believe in Bigfoot, that's all right, too. It's the same with all the monsters in this book. There is no proof that they are real. But a lot of people say they have seen these monsters.

You can decide for yourself. Does America really have its very own monsters?

The Skunk Ape

The best-known Bigfoot reports come from the Northwest part of the country. But there are tales of Bigfoot-like creatures all over North America. The thing has different names in different places.

In Canada it is called Sasquatch. In Missouri it is the Missouri Monster or Mo-Mo. In parts of Arkansas it is called the Fouke Monster. That is because it was seen near the town of Fouke.

In Florida it is called the Skunk Ape. It got that name because it looks like an ape and smells terrible. Often people smell it before they see it.

A young woman tells this story. In 1966 she was driving down a lonely road near Brooksville, Florida. Her car had a flat tire. She got out to fix the tire. She smelled something terrible. Then she heard a noise. She turned. There was a huge hairy thing standing by the road. It was looking right at her. She was frightened.

Then another car came along. The thing walked back into the woods. The young woman stopped the passing car and escaped.

Ralph "Bud" Chambers of Elfers, Florida, saw the thing twice. He said it was about seven feet tall. Its smell made him sick. The second time he saw it, Chambers was with his dog. The dog attacked it. The thing barely noticed. It just walked back down the road that led to the swamp. The dog didn't follow. Neither did Chambers.

In 1973 there were a large number of Skunk

Ape reports. One man said the thing ran out in front of his car. He hit it. It limped off to the side of the road. The man did not go back to see if it was badly hurt. He just drove away as fast as he could.

The police looked into the case. They said the man hit something. They didn't know what.

No one has ever been able to catch a Skunk Ape. No one has caught any of the other Bigfoot-like creatures. Are they still out there?

One night you and your family may be driving along a dark road. You may see a strange figure at the side of the road. It may look a little like a man and a little like an ape. If I were you, I wouldn't stop.

Washington's Demon Cat

Most of America's monsters live deep in the woods. Some live in dark, cold lakes. But one of them is supposed to live right in Washington, D.C. In fact, it is said to live in the Capitol Building itself. The creature is called the Demon Cat.

The Capitol Building is where Congress meets. Beneath the building are basements and tunnels. This is where the Demon Cat is found. Visitors never report seeing this monster because they come in groups and do not go into the tunnels. The peo-

ple who see the cat are mostly members of the Capitol Police Force. They are on guard in the tunnels at night, and alone.

This is how one guard described his meeting with the Demon Cat. It was a winter night. The guard was walking through the cold, dimly lit

halls. He saw a small cat with strange, glowing eyes. As the cat walked toward him, it grew larger and larger. It grew to the size of a tiger. Its purring changed to a roar.

The guard was frozen with fear. The Demon Cat stopped just a few feet from him. It was ready to spring. As the cat leaped toward him, the frightened guard covered his face with his arms. He screamed. But nothing happened. When the guard looked, the Demon Cat was not there.

That's the way meetings with the Demon Cat go. It grows to a huge size. Then, just as it leaps, it disappears. It is very scary. An elderly guard is said to have died of a heart attack after meeting the monster cat.

Some say the Demon Cat is a warning. They say it is seen when something terrible is about to happen to the country. It is said to appear before a war or the death of a president.

The Flatwoods Monster

In 1952 everybody was talking about Flying Saucers. Today we call them UFOs. They are supposed to be flying ships from outer space. Most scientists don't believe there are such things. But a lot of people do.

On September 12, 1952, something bright flashed through the sky near Flatwoods, West Virginia. The glowing thing seemed to crash on a hilltop. A group of young people went to see what had happened.

They climbed quickly up the hill. At the top
they saw something. It scared them very badly.
They ran back down the hill and called the sheriff.

They told the sheriff they had seen "a monster."
One said, "It was ten feet tall. It had a bright
green body and a blood-red face." Another said, "It
was worse then Frankenstein."

The sheriff and men with guns went up the hill.
They didn't find anything. The sheriff didn't
think there was any kind of monster at all. He

thought the young people saw an animal in a tree. With all the talk about Flying Saucers, they got excited. They were scared and just thought they saw a monster.

But the people stuck to their story. They told it to the newspapers. They appeared on radio. They were on TV. The Flatwoods Monster became very famous.

But no one ever saw it again.

Goatman

GOATMAN WAS HERE

That can sometimes be seen on walls and sidewalks in Prince Georges County, Maryland. Some people don't believe the Goatman story. Others do, and they are scared. Goatman is half-man, half-goat. The upper part of his body is like a man's. The lower part is covered with fur. His feet have hoofs like a goat.

The creature lives deep in the woods. Not many people see him. But sometimes they do. When a

car is on a lonely road, Goatman will rush out of the woods. He jumps on the car. Some say he carries an ax. He beats the car with it. Others say he just bangs on the car with his fists. No one stays around long enough to find out. They do not know why he is so angry.

Who or what is Goatman? There are different stories. Some say he is a kind of animal. They say he has lived in the woods as long as anyone can remember. A better story says that he was a scientist. He worked at a government center in Maryland. The scientist was doing experiments on goats. Then something went wrong. He was turned into a half-man, half-goat.

Because he looked so terrible, he ran off into the woods to hide. Living alone, he has come to hate people. That is why he sometimes attacks cars.

The White River Monster

The White River runs past the town of Newport, Arkansas. Just south of town is a bridge. Cloyce Warren was standing on the bridge one day. He saw a lot of foam and bubbles in the water. Something was out there. It was over 30 feet long. Its color was dark gray.

"It had a long snake-like body," said Warren. "It was hard to make out what the front looked like. But it was awful large. I've never seen anything like it. I was scared to death."

"It" was the White River Monster. People around Newport call it Whitey. They have been seeing it since the 1930s.

Near Newport the White River is 60 feet deep. The water is dark, and dangerous to swim in. Something very large could hide in that water.

The first man to report the White River Mon-

ster was Bramlett Bateman. He owned land near the river. Bateman said he had seen the monster many times. A lot of people wanted to get a look at it. There were so many that Bateman fenced off part of his land. He charged people a quarter to stand and look. Visitors still go to Newport today.

Most people see nothing. A few see a snake-like

body. Ernest Denks saw the head. He said it had a huge mouth. It also had a bone sticking out of the middle of its forehead.

Usually Whitey stays away from people. But not always. In the summer of 1971, Ollie Richardson and Joe Dupree went fishing. Something came up under their boat. The boat was lifted right up out of the water. It was turned sideways in the river. The two men didn't see what had lifted them up. But they were sure it was the monster. What else could it have been?

There is also the story about a man who took a boat up the river. He went toward a spot where the monster was often seen. Later the boat was found empty. The man was never found. No one knows what happened. Lots of people say the White River Monster got him.

The Beast of Busco

The town of Churubusco, Indiana, has a festival in honor of a monster. The monster is Oscar, the "Beast of Busco." He is the biggest snapping turtle anybody has ever heard of.

The story started in 1948. A farmer named Gale Harris had a large lake on his land. He went fishing in the lake. Harris noticed there were not so many fish. And a flock of ducks was gone.

Things got worse. A cow disappeared. The cow went to the lake to drink. The hoofprints led to the edge of the water. No prints led back.

33

Something had killed the fish, the ducks, and a cow. It was something huge, and hungry.

It turned out to be a giant-size snapping turtle. Some said it was as big as a table. Others said it was even bigger.

People from all around came to Harris's lake. They wanted to see the monster turtle. They wanted to catch it. And they tried. They went af-

ter it with hooks, traps, and guns. Oscar always
got away.

But Harris studied the big turtle's habits. One
day when Oscar was asleep the farmer slipped a
chain around the turtle's middle. He attached the
other end of the chain to four strong horses.

The horses pulled. Oscar dug his claws into the
mud. The more the horses pulled, the more Oscar

dug. Who would give up first, Oscar or the horses? Neither. The chain gave up. It broke. The horses fell forward. Oscar slid back into the water.

Ever since, the town has remembered the great battle by having the Turtle Days festival. Visitors can buy toy turtles and turtle T-shirts. They can eat candy in the shape of a turtle. There are all sorts of foods named after turtles for sale.

What about Oscar? He hasn't been seen for a while. Some say he died from the tug-of-war with the horses. Others say he is just resting. Turtles live a long time. No one thinks that you should go swimming in Harris's lake.

The Thunderbird

The American Indians told stories of the Thunderbird. It was bigger than any other bird. It was so big it could blot out the sun.

The Thunderbird is just a tale. Or is it? Some people think there really was a giant bird. At one time it lived in America. This huge bird was the reason for Thunderbird stories. Some people think there are giant birds around today.

One story says that a Thunderbird was shot near Tombstone, Arizona, in 1886. The dead bird was put up on a barn. Its wings were spread out. Six men stood in front of it. They spread out their arms, with their fingers touching. That way the men could cover a length of 35 feet. That's how long the bird's wings were supposed to be. Any known bird has wings under ten feet long.

A picture of the six men in front of the monster bird was taken. The trouble is that nobody can find that picture.

There are a lot of stories of airplanes meeting a giant bird. The pilot of a small plane thought another plane was following him. Then he saw that the other "airplane" was flapping its wings. It wasn't a plane at all. It was a Thunderbird.

Then there are stories of airplanes that crash after a monster bird hits them. Blood, feathers, and claw marks are found on the planes.

But these are all just stories. There is no way to prove they are true. Are there really huge Thunderbirds flying around?

Mothman

Point Pleasant is a small town in West Virginia. Something scared a lot of people there. The "something" was about six feet tall. It looked like a man. But it had huge wings. It could fly at 100 miles an hour.

People called it Mothman.

The story began on the night of November 15, 1966. Two couples were driving just outside of town. The road was lonely. They saw a figure by the side of the road. The figure seemed to have on a gray cape. But it wasn't a cape. The thing had wings folded around its body. It flew straight up into the air. It hung over the car.

The people were scared. They drove back to town. The driver swears he hit 100 miles per hour. The flying creature kept up with them. Just before town it turned off.

Other people said they saw Mothman. They said it had bright red eyes. "Those eyes," said Connie Carpenter. "I couldn't take my own eyes off them. It's a wonder I didn't have a wreck." The rest of its face was pretty awful, too, she said.

A family said that Mothman walked up on their porch. It looked in the window. They ran out the back door.

People who saw Mothman said their own eyes burned afterward. Many said they couldn't forget it. They had bad dreams for weeks.

After a time Mothman disappeared. No one ever found out what it was. But there were plenty of ideas.

Some scientists said it was just a big bird. It might have been a crane or a stork. They said that people were frightened. They couldn't tell how big the thing really was.

Others did not believe the scientists. They said that UFOs had been seen near Point Pleasant. Mothman might have come from one of the UFOs.

We may never know for sure what Mothman was.

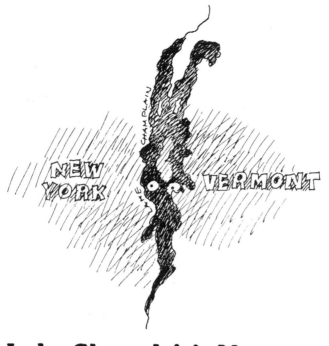

Lake Champlain's Monster

People call it Champ. They say it lives in Lake Champlain. That is a large lake between New York and Vermont, near Canada. Champ is the most famous water monster in America today.

There are stories about monsters in many large lakes in America. For a long time Champ was just another story. Then Sandra Mansi took a picture of "something" in the lake. It was July, 1977. She thought it was the monster. It had a long neck. It had a small head.

"I was scared to death," she said. "I felt I shouldn't be there."

The picture was taken to scientists. They said it was not a fake. But the picture wasn't very clear. It might have been the head and neck of the monster. Or maybe it was just a big stick in the water.

More and more people have been seeing Champ

since 1977. They come from all over the world to Lake
Champlain. They want to try to see the monster. Tele-
vision and newspaper people come to look for Champ.
Everyone gets excited.

But still the scientists aren't sure. In 1981 they had
a meeting about Champ. The meeting was held near
Lake Champlain. The scientists heard all the stories.

They talked to people who said they had seen Champ.

Some scientists thought the monster was a whale. Others said it might be a giant animal from the Age of the Dinosaurs. Some said it was all made-up. Still others were just not sure.

Every summer more and more people visit Lake Champlain. They look for Champ. They stand on the shore and stare at the water. They go out in boats. Some even fly over the lake in helicopters.

Not everyone who looks for Champ thinks they see him. But everybody has a good time looking. America enjoys its very own monsters.